simple

small group study

The Christian Life
Doesn't Have to Be
Complicated

Robert J. Morgan

randall house
114 Bush Rd | Nashville, TN 37217 | randallhouse.com

Published by Randall House Publications
114 Bush Road
Nashville, TN 37217

Printed in the United States of America

ISBN-13: 978-0-89265-689-9

contents

introduction

Simplicity seems to be a rare commodity in this world full of complication and clutter. Many seem to feel that the Christian life adds to the complication. However, the basics of Christianity can be explained in simple terms. This six-week small group study is my effort to help new believers gain a clear picture of the Christian life. I also want to aid long-time believers who are interested in rediscovering the basics of their faith. So turn the pages to encounter basic Bible truths in understandable terms, using personal, everyday examples of the truths being explored. Numerous Bible passages will further clarify the ABC's of Christianity—assurance, baptism, church, devotions, and evangelism.

May the Lord bless you with the simplicity of His grace as you study and grow in Christ!

Robert J. Morgan

week 1

Is Salvation *Really* Simple?

W hen Henry David Thoreau made his mark, simplicity was already
en vogue. His basic rule for healthy living? "Simplify! Simplify!"
Two hundred years later finds that mantra proliferated seemingly
everywhere. The ideal of a simple life, a simple schedule, a simple diet, a simple
relationship is ever set before the modern citizen. But what does simple really
mean?

1. In your own words, define *simple*:

Simple (Adj)-

1. easy to understand, deal with, use.

2. not so elaborate or artificial; plain

page 2.

not complicated.

2. Now consult a dictionary and/or thesaurus; what are the "official" meanings of *simple*?

No doubt it is the messiness and complexities of sin that makes simplicity so appealing; yet many find a simpler schedule does not produce joy or peace or anything lasting. The true source for such is found—as you've discovered—in relationship with Jesus Christ, the Redeemer.

3. Yet, how many times have people (even you) protested that salvation is too complicated, the Christian life too demanding and complex? Are these valid points? Are these just excuses? What do you think?

They are excuses that come from people that don't want to listen to the Holy Spirit and change their old ways

The Christian life is simple. No, not always *easy*, but remember—Christianity doesn't have to be complicated. We tend to make things harder than they are because, after all, life is unimaginably complex.

If anyone should be an expert in simplicity, it's the Christian. It's not that we're simple-minded; we deal with the deepest truths under heaven. But we are simple of heart and habit. And while our beliefs are deep enough to challenge the world's greatest thinkers, they're plain enough for children to understand.

4. Read the following verses. What do you learn about God and the simplicity of the Christian life?

    a. Matthew 18:2–3

The christian life is so easy a child can do it. Absolute faith like a child.

b. 1 Corinthians 14:33

That when following God you
have a sense of peace.

c. 2 Corinthians 1:12

We weren't saved by us. If we
were Jesus wouldn't have had
to come and die for us. He (God)
sent His son to die our death so
we could have a life with Him.

week 1 day 2

W hile our salvation cost Christ enormously, He willingly and whole-heartedly accomplished the task. He made redemption simple to acquire.

1. Write out Romans 10:9 and 5:1, which present the "formula" for a right relationship with God.

Romans 10:9. If thou shall confess with your mouth
that Jesus is Lord & believe it in their heart you shall
be saved.

2. Why do you think some scoff at this path to salvation? What is so offensive about it?

They maybe believe that their salvation
is temporary, that their next sin will
send them to hell.

3. What do you find appealing about God's plan for salvation?

It's so easy. a cave man can do it?

LOL.

4. Write your salvation story: How did God pursue you? When did you begin to understand His love for you? How did you react to His provision, kindness, and care?

I had been going to church for 5-6 years. It was just after I made it in the youth room. I pulled my youth pastor aside and asked him how I get saved. and he prayed with me and I repeated his prayer. I was so excited to be a part of God's family, after church was over we ran downstairs and told my mom. She cried.

Ask a group of chemists to describe water. They'll tell you that a water molecule is made up of two hydrogen atoms and one oxygen atom, and it can be split into its constituent elements through electrolysis, causing the water molecules to dissociate into H+ and OH- ions, which are pulled toward the cathode and anode respectively.

Ask a group of children about water, and they'll tell you it's something you drink when you're thirsty. Both answers happen to be correct.

Ask a philosopher or theologian about Christianity and you may get an esoteric answer that may be correct in every respect. But you don't have to be a chemist to enjoy a cool drink of water, nor must you be a canonized saint to enjoy the living water offered by Jesus Christ. The more we study the Bible, of course, the deeper and richer we'll be; but Christianity is best enjoyed simply.

Success in life comes from sticking with the basics of the Bible, the ABCs of the Christian faith, namely:

ASSURANCE—How can I know for sure?

BAPTISM—Why should I get wet?

CHURCH—What's it got to offer?

DEVOTIONS—How can I stay close to God?

EVANGELISM—How can I share my faith with others?

1. As a starting point and without any further study, how would you answer the following questions? (Please, please, do not stress or worry about getting the "right" answer. These questions are a starting point for discussion. At this point in the study, there are no correct answers.)

a. Before you became a Christ-follower, what were you taught about the path to heaven?

you had to be good, do the right thing, help others,

b. How can you know for sure that you are going to heaven when you die?

If you did what you could to be the best you could be and helped others you'd go to heaven

c. Before you became a Christ-follower, what were you taught about baptism?

d. Based on your knowledge and understanding right now, what is the purpose of baptism?

Its an outward showing of an inward change that you made. It shows your fellow christians you are commiting your life to God

Some of my earliest childhood memories are sitting on the hard pews of our church in Elizabethton, Tennessee. I remember seeing my dad and mom up in the choir. I recall our pastor, Rev. Winford R. Floyd, preaching the Bible to us. He would often weep during his sermons, and he preached with intelligence, passion, and conviction. I don't remember many of his individual sermons, but the cumulative effect of hearing him preach Sunday after Sunday for all the years of my childhood was profound.

I remember how we would often close the service with baptisms. After the sermon and the invitation, Pastor Floyd would excuse himself, call for those who were to be baptized to follow him, and then they all retired to the dressing rooms while the rest of us sang "Shall We Gather at the River." In a few minutes, they would come into the baptismal pool to give public demonstration of their faith in Christ.

I recall hearing people stand to share their testimonies. There was an older woman named Pearl McGee who sat right behind us most Sundays. She wasn't a particularly outgoing woman, but occasionally she would stand to share a word of testimony; and she always spoke with so much passion she almost seemed angry. She was so vehement about what Christ had done for her that my father tried to avoid sitting directly in front of her. He sometimes complained that in her excitement she would pound his shoulders while testifying.

1. What about for you? What memories and/or emotions stir when you hear the word *church*?

sense of security - family - love. non-judgement.

2. In your opinion, what is the church? What is its role?

The church are a ~~bunch~~ body of Christians

To support, other christians and help guide those that may not know christ.

While worshiping together and living life together with other believers is an outward, necessary expression of our belonging to God's family, personal Bible study—often called devotions and prayer—is a private, inward nurturing of our relationship with Christ.

3. Do you find regular Bible study and prayer a difficult habit to practice? Why or why not?

Yes, I struggle with my time management. and a lot of the time my time w/ God suffers when I'm busy or had a long day.

I f you are a Christ-follower, it is likely someone—or a variety of people—told you about Jesus Christ. That explanation of God's story of salvation, whether in tidbits or in its entirety, is called evangelism and can take seemingly endless forms and uses numerous mediums. Simply, evangelism is communicating the gospel to others.

1. List the people who were influential in your conversion to Christ. Explain how and what they shared about God.

Christ Fingerlow - He prayed with me.

2. What can you learn about evangelism from these people?

3. What do you believe is your role in evangelism?

Now that you have completed Week 1 take time to write a prayer of thanksgiving for your salvation.

Dear God,

In Jesus' name, Amen

week 2

Assurance: How Can I Know for Sure?

The tires on my car had seen better days. When on a wet or snow-covered road, they sort of slid and squealed around corners. I wanted new, longwearing tires that really gripped the road. The tire salesman assured me that he had just what I wanted, and that they were guaranteed to last the lifetime of the car. That sounded reassuring to me! After the tires were installed, I took a test drive. What a difference! The tires were great, gripping the road like Velcro. But just a month after I bought the "lifetime" guaranteed tires, one of them developed a leak and went completely flat. Although the tire was replaced, I didn't have much confidence in the "lifetime" guarantee for the other tires.

I'm sure you can recall similar incidents where something—or someone—didn't live up to what was promised. A furnace didn't heat, a refrigerator didn't cool, or a person didn't keep his or her word. After a while, we begin to suspect most guarantees and assurances that are offered. Based on our experiences, we doubt whether anything is absolutely sure.

Sometimes we transfer those doubts to our faith. We may ask if we can be absolutely sure, beyond a shadow of doubt, that we are going to heaven when we die. We may doubt whether we're good enough, or worry that we have done something that makes us unworthy of being a Christian. This isn't an uncommon experience. Many thousands of faithful church people, who have received Christ, are unsure of their salvation. But there's no reason to doubt or fear—Christians can be *absolutely* sure of going to heaven.

1. Read the Bible verses below. What do you learn about the writers' attitudes concerning the Lord of salvation?

    a. Job 19:25–26

    b. Psalm 20:6

c. Romans 8:38–39

d. 2 Timothy 1:12

2. What do the Bible verses listed in the previous question mean
   to you? How do they impact your view of your own relationship
   with Jesus Christ?

Assurance of salvation isn't a matter of whether or not you feel saved. Nor is it a matter of knowing the precise time and place that you became a Christian. What's important is what God has done and what He tells us in His Word, "Believe on the Lord Jesus Christ, and you will be saved" (Acts 16:31). There's no doubt or uncertainty about salvation in these words of God. The Bible uses clear, direct words of certainty and assurance concerning salvation.

There are two important questions to ask and answer. Do you *know* Christ? And do you *know that you know* Christ? In other words: "Are you saved, and do you have assurance of your salvation?" The apostle John, one of Jesus' disciples and author of the gospel and the epistles of John, helps us answer these questions.

1. John 20:30–31 is the purpose statement for the book of John. What do you identify as that purpose?

2. Why is a salvation centered in Jesus Christ so significant?

Our salvation is centered on Jesus and what He has done. John 20:30–31 presents three names for this Savior.

First, He is Jesus. The name means *Jehovah saves.*

3. Based on Romans 4:25, how did Jesus "save"?

The whole teaching of the Bible is this: The God who created us is very powerful and very pure, but all of us have brought shame and disgrace upon ourselves. We are all sinners, and sinners cannot inhabit God's presence in eternity. So God became a man—Jesus Christ—born through the womb of a virgin; He Himself was pure, sinless, and perfect. When He died on the cross, He bore the penalty and punishment for our sins so that in Him we might have forgiveness and eternal life, not on the basis of our own merits, but on the basis of His righteousness, His death on the cross, and His resurrection from the grave.

Second, He is the Christ. This is the English translation of the Greek work *Christos*, which was the Greek term for the Hebrew word *Messiah*. It literally means *Anointed One*. Long before Jesus was born in Bethlehem, the Old Testament prophets predicted that a Messiah would be sent into the world, anointed by God, to provide the human race with hope, heaven, forgiveness of sin, and everlasting life. Seven centuries before Christ was born, the prophet Isaiah wrote, "The Spirit of the Sovereign LORD is on me, because the LORD *has anointed me* to proclaim good news to the poor" (Isaiah 61:1, NIV, emphasis mine). He predicted the coming of the Anointed One, the Christ.

Third, Jesus is the Son of God. This is a classic title for Jesus, but many people underestimate its meaning because we don't hear those three words—*Son of God*—as they were understood in Bible times. We take them literally, but among the Hebrews it was an idiomatic phrase. They often used *father*-and-*son* terminology not just to convey lineage, but characteristics. To say "son of " was to mean "possessing the distinctives of." Thus, when Jesus called Himself the Son of God, He was emphasizing His god-ness. Jesus was not less than God—He was and is God.

4. Read John 3:16; how does this verse show salvation as centered in Jesus Christ?

The truth about salvation is conveyed through the Bible. It is a book that can be carried with us, opened at any time to be read, studied, and memorized.

5. What does 2 Timothy 3:16 reveal about the Bible, making it unlike any other book?

6. If the Bible—God's own words—clearly presents salvation through belief in Jesus Christ and all that He is, how can these truths combat doubt and fear about assurance of salvation?

The Bible tells us that Christ died for our sins and that because of His death we are forgiven and will go to heaven when we die. We claim our forgiveness and eternal life (salvation) by faith. The book of John is very important in conveying this wonderful truth. It has the purpose of telling us that our salvation, centered in Christ and proclaimed in the Bible, is claimed by faith alone. "But these are written that you may believe that Jesus is the Christ, the Son of God, and that believing you may have life in His name" (John 20:31). The main theme of John's gospel is *believing and belief.*

1. How is the message of salvation conveyed in the Bible verses below? How does that message apply to you?

   a. John 1:11–12

b. John 5:24

c. John 6:29

d. John 6:40

e. John 6:47

f. John 11:25–26

2. The most important question we can ever ask is: What must I do to be saved? How do these verses answer that question:

   a. Acts 16:31

   b. Ephesians 2:8–9

   c. Romans 10:9

What does it mean to believe in Jesus? It means to acknowledge Christ as Lord and to place your life in His hands.

Years ago, my wife and I were traveling in New Mexico with a friend. On Sunday morning, we went to church and the pastor preached the sermon on this theme. At the end of his message, he told a story I had heard several times before, and I thought to myself, *That's such an old story that I can't believe he used it. Could he not find a newer and better one?* But later, the friend traveling with us said, "That was the best illustration I've ever heard of being saved by faith. I've never understood that truth as clearly as I do now."

So, with apologies to my preacher friend in New Mexico, let me tell you this well-worn story.

In the 1850s, there was a French daredevil with the stage name of Blondin who made several visits to Niagara Falls where he would thrill the crowds by performing feats on a high-wire stretched over the falls.

One of his favorite stunts was to cross the tightrope pushing a wheelbarrow. On one occasion, he stopped at the edge of the falls to chat with the pop-eyed crowds who had gathered to watch him.

"Do you believe I can walk over the falls on this little rope?" he asked. A man in the crowd said, "Yes, certainly."

"Do you believe I can walk over the falls on this rope pushing a wheelbarrow?"

"Yes, I do believe that!" replied the man.

"Do you believe I can walk over the falls pushing a wheelbarrow with someone in it?"

"Yes," said the man. "I've seen you do it before."

"Then, kind sir," challenged the daredevil, "would you mind assisting me by getting into the wheelbarrow?"

To which the man answered: "Not on your life!"

True saving faith means getting into the wheelbarrow. It isn't just a matter of intellectual assent but of life commitment. It means that we know the content of the gospel; we believe it with our minds; and we are giving ourselves to it with our hearts and lives.

I believe the best way to do that is through prayer. When I'm with someone who wants to become a Christian, I lead him or her in a simple prayer expressing his or her faith, something like this:

"Dear God, I confess my sins to You and ask for Your forgiveness. I do believe that Jesus Christ died for my sins and rose again to give me everlasting life. I here and now give Him my life and ask Him to become my Savior and Lord."

How do you know that you were born physically? You are breathing right now, you have a birth certificate, and you bear some kind of family resemblance. When we become Christians, we are "born again" into God's family.

These same three tests can help you know you are born again. So how can you know that you are a Christian? First, you're breathing. For Christians, the Holy Spirit is like oxygen. If you have the Holy Spirit living in you, you can know you are saved.

1. What do these verses tell you about the Holy Spirit?

   a. 1 John 4:13

b. Romans 8:16

c. Galatians 4:6

2. How does the Holy Spirit work in your life?

Second, we can know we have been saved because we have a "birth certificate."
When we are born into God's family (become a Christian) our names are recorded
in the heavenly records (Revelation 21:27). Our birth certificate is also the Bible—
the Bible tells us we are saved through Jesus, and the Bible is reliable no matter
how we may feel.

3. Have you given your life to Jesus, but still have doubts?
   Memorize 1 John 5:11–12 and believe it with all your being.
   Write it below, and let it become your memory verse.

Third, we can know we are Christians because we have a family likeness. We take on the characteristics and image of Jesus. We begin to grow in our resemblance to Him—people can see Jesus in us.

4. Read 1 John and note how you can reflect Jesus in your life.

   a. 1 John 1:6

   b. 1 John 2:3

c. 1 John 2:5

d. 1 John 2:29

e. 1 John 3:14

5. How will others know you have Christ in your life? List three
   areas you will work on this week:

1. Write out 2 Corinthians 13:5.

The Bible teaches that God is love, and His love is forever; it never ends. Because of that love, He gave His only Son to die for your sins. As a Christian, you want to reflect God's love in your life. Your growing love of God and others is another proof that you have been saved.

Take some quiet time to honestly examine what you do, say, and how you live. Has there been a change in your behavior as a result of giving your life to Christ? Do you still have some lingering doubts?

2. Write a prayer for guidance. Ask the Holy Spirit to help you live each day joyfully, knowing that you have been saved and have eternal life waiting for you.

3. Write out John 20:31 and commit to memorizing it.

As we close Week 2 write out a prayer of praise for the assurance of salvation God provides.

Dear God,

In Jesus' name, Amen

week 3

Baptism: Why Should I Get Wet?

The rite or ritual of baptism is often most intriguing to people who visit a local church. It's so personal and unusual, yet so public, that those new to church naturally raise their eyebrows.

1. If you have attended a baptism, what details about the ritual do you remember?

2. What do you think is significant and/or unusual about baptism?

The words *baptize* and *baptism* occur exactly 100 times in the New Testament, so we know it's an important subject in the Bible. The first time we find this word in Scripture is at the beginning of the New Testament in Matthew's gospel. Before Jesus Christ began His ministry, He was preceded by John the Baptist, "the Baptizer," who was His forerunner, sent by God to prepare the way.

3. Read Matthew 3:1–6, noting what you learn about John's ministry.

In some ways, this was a new thing in the Bible, a new habit or ritual. Although the Old Testament contained instructions regarding various washings and cleansing ceremonies in Jewish worship, there was no Old Testament precedent, commandment, or example regarding baptism.

On the other hand, this ordinance was not actually "invented" by John. Symbolic immersion was well-known in the days of Christ. Archaeologists have found many ritual basins called *mikvahs*, dating from the first century that were used by Jewish people when preparing for worship.

It appears, then, that while baptism is not found in the Old Testament, there were some customs pre-dating John the Baptist that were roughly similar to our New Testament practice of baptism; and when John the Baptist came baptizing, he adapted this tradition and gave it a new meaning. He said to the people of his day, in effect: "If you want to be a true Jew in your heart, if you want to be God's holy people, if you really want to belong to Him, you need to repent of your sins. And baptism in water is an outward symbol of that inward attitude of repentance, change, and cleansing." It was just then that a most remarkable thing happened.

The only Person in the history of the world who needed no repentance, being sinless and pure, showed up to be baptized.

4. Read Matthew 3:13–17. What do you find interesting and/or astounding about this account?

After the baptism of Jesus, little more is said about baptism in the Gospels. There is a suggestion in John 4 that the disciples of Jesus baptized those coming to Him, but references to baptism are sparse until the end of our Lord's earthly ministry when He gave us a special commandment just before He returned to heaven. We call it the Great Commission.

5. Write out Matthew 28:18–20. What do you learn about baptism's importance from these verses?

6. How do the Bible passages from this day's study make baptism more understandable to you?

After Jesus ascended into heaven, the disciples spent 10 days praying and waiting before the Lord, and then on the Day of Pentecost, the Holy Spirit fell from heaven upon them as they were gathered in the Upper Room, and that is the birth of the church. Immediately Peter started preaching the gospel, and notice what happened on that day.

1. Immediately after the Holy Spirit's appearance, Peter began telling others about the gospel. According to Acts 2:41, what happened that day?

Later in Acts 8, we have a glimpse into the way this worked in the experience of one of the early evangelists.

2. Read Acts 8:26–40, noting what you learn about baptism.

This passage reveals several things about baptism:

• Baptism is biblical. The Bible commands and commends it. New Testament Christians were baptized as a symbol of making a decision to follow Christ.

• Baptism is basic. It's one of the first things that happens after a person becomes a Christian.

• Baptism is beneficial. There's something about baptism that's good for the person being baptized and for the church—a feeling of rejoicing.

3. What questions do you want to ask your pastor or small group leader about baptism?

We have explored many biblical and historical reasons for baptism, but some questions still remain. What exactly does baptism mean today? Why is baptism the great, biblical sign of conversion to Christ?

1. Read Matthew 20:20–22 and Luke 12:50. What do you understand Jesus to mean?

Why did Jesus select this ritual—baptism in water? Perhaps because it was such a powerful symbol of the other baptism He would face—the real baptism.

The *only real baptism* took place when Jesus died on the cross and rose from the dead. Baptism is synonymous with the death and resurrection of Christ. The death, burial, and resurrection of Jesus are the whole essence of the gospel. When Jesus spoke of His baptism into suffering, it was for the sins of the entire world, your sins and my sins, that we might be forgiven and become children of God.

2. How do these Bible passages affirm that truth?

    a. 1 Corinthians 15:3–4

    b. 2 Corinthians 5:18

c. Colossians 1:19

d. 1 Peter 2:24; 3:18

e. 1 John 2:2

The death, burial, and resurrection of Jesus Christ, then, is the ultimate baptism in Scripture. There is only one real baptism in this sense because no other name exists under heaven whereby to be saved. There is no other Savior, and no other answer to sin and death.

3. How does this truth strengthen your faith?

The *only real baptism* took place when Jesus died on the cross and rose from the dead. Baptism is synonymous with the death and resurrection of Christ. The death, burial, and resurrection of Jesus are the whole essence of the gospel. When Jesus spoke of His baptism into suffering, it was for the sins of the entire world, your sins and my sins, that we might be forgiven and become children of God.

When Jesus stood in the water, He was standing upright in the river, just as He would later hang upright for the sins of the world. When He was lowered into the water, it was symbolic of His death and burial. When He was raised out of the water, it was a pre-enactment of His resurrection from the tomb.

Think of it! The first thing Jesus did in His earthly ministry was to provide a vivid symbol of what would take place at the climax of His earthly years. He was previewing His passion—His death, burial, and resurrection. He was telling the world in advance what He was going to do for us on the cross.

The second symbolic baptism is ours—the ordinance of baptism we observe Sunday after Sunday in our churches, and it coveys a similar meaning. When Jesus was baptized, it was in *anticipation* of what He was going to do. When we are baptized, it is in *commemoration* of what He has already done. It announces to the entire world that we are identifying ourselves publicly with the death, burial, and resurrection of Christ.

1. What does Romans 6:3–4 teach you about our relationship with Christ in baptism?

Jesus' baptism in water *looked forward* to the cross; our baptism in water *looks back* at the cross and what Christ has done for us. Baptism is a testimony. It sends a signal to others. It's a way of preaching a wordless sermon that communicates your new life to others.

2. Read the following Bible verses, stating beside each how your baptism identifies you as a Christ-follower.

 a. Romans 6:4

 b. Acts 22:16

 c. Revelation 1:5

 d. Acts 1:4–5

e. 1 Corinthians 10:1–2

f. 1 Corinthians 12:12–13

3. How are you conveying that message in your life?

nother question that often arises is this one: Is baptism necessary for salvation? If I sincerely ask Christ to be my Lord and Savior, but I'm not baptized, am I really going to heaven? There are some Scripture verses that can be interpreted as indicating that baptism is necessary for salvation, and many Christian groups throughout church history and in our own day believe that.

First, baptism is not necessary for salvation. The dying thief on the cross went to be with the Lord in Paradise though it was impossible for him to be baptized in water.

1. What do these verses teach you about the requirements for salvation?

   a. Titus 3:5

b. Ephesians 2:8–9

In Acts 10, the apostle Peter went to the city of Caesarea where some Gentiles (non-Jews) wanted to become Christians. This was a novel and controversial thing because until then Christianity had been more-or-less contained within Judaism. Peter went and preached the gospel to them. Read what he said in verses 36–43.

2. What happened next (verses 44–48)?

Note the order of events. They heard the gospel and believed and were saved. The Holy Spirit came upon them. By the power of the Holy Spirit, they became members of the family of God.

Then Peter said, in effect, "These people are Christians now. These people have Jesus in them. They have the Holy Spirit. Furthermore, the Spirit has already baptized them into His church. They are now part of the body of Christ. Who, then, can forbid them from taking the outward step symbolizing that? Who can forbid their being baptized with water?"

So baptism is not necessary for salvation. But there's another side to the coin. Baptism is *not necessary* for salvation, yet baptism is *not optional*. To the best of our observation and knowledge, every person in the New Testament who decided to follow Jesus Christ was baptized. It is a universal command for Christians throughout history and around the world. Acts 2:38 says, "Repent, and be baptized, every one of you." There are no examples in the Bible of unbaptized believers, except the thief on the cross. It was a universal anticipation and joy.

3. Have you committed your life to Jesus Christ as your Lord and Savior? Do you want to be baptized or re-baptized? Think it through carefully and express your feelings as you make this wonderful decision.

If you want to be baptized, or if you want to talk with someone about it, call your pastor or your church office and make an appointment to talk with someone about this as soon as possible.

4. Write out Romans 6:4 and commit it to memory.

Now that Week 3 has come to a close take a moment to write out a prayer for boldness to share your faith with others.

Dear God,

In Jesus' name, Amen

week 4

Church: What's It Got to Offer?

1. How do you define church? Using the acrostic below, describe the church. Find a word or phrase that begins with each letter in the word *church*.

C

H

U

R

C

H

Two friends completed this puzzle as well—Mike and Bryan. Mike's acrostic looked like this:

Cathedral

House of worship

Urban landmark

Resting place

Chapel

Holy place

Bryan's acrostic looked like this:

Charlie

Hattie

Ursula

Ralph

Christi

Howard

The difference between the two men's acrostics was that Mike associated a building with the word *church*, and Bryan associated people with the word.

2. What do you look at more closely in a church—the building or people? Why?

The most basic thing we can say about "church" is that the church is not a building. It's a group of people who know Jesus Christ as Savior. They may meet in a building, or they may meet in a cave or under a tree; but the building itself is not the church. It's simply the meeting place for Christians.

The word *church* occurs 110 times in the New Testament, and it's a translation of the Greek word *ekklesia*, from the prefix *ek*, meaning *out*, and the Greek verb meaning *to call*. The word literally means "the called out ones," Christians being those who have been called out of sin to become members of a new family and citizens of a new kingdom.

No, the church isn't perfect; and yes, it has its share of hypocrites. Every church is made up of people from various backgrounds, possessing various levels of maturity or immaturity. In fact, every single Christian on earth is a hypocrite to some extent for our beliefs are richer than our behavior. We're pardoned, but we aren't yet perfect. We're under construction, but construction sites are seldom pretty spots.

3. Read Acts 20:28 and Colossians 1:18.

    a. What is meant by "the church" in these Bible verses?

    b. What do these verses tell you about the importance of the church to Jesus Christ?

    c. How does that make you feel about being part of the church?

After Jesus Christ rose from the dead, His followers expected that He would go on to conquer the entire known world and restore the kingdom to Israel. They had no idea that thousands of years would pass between Jesus' resurrection and second coming.

1. Read Acts 1:6–11 and identify how the disciples questioned Jesus about His intentions and how Jesus answered their questions.

When Jesus ascended into heaven, the disciples were so stunned that they needed an angel to jolt them back to their senses. At the time, there were more than one hundred followers of Jesus and they met together in an upper room. They stayed there for 10 days in seclusion, waiting and praying. Then, on Pentecost, everything changed and the church was born.

2. Read about the beginning of the church in Acts 2:1–11. Imagine you were there. What did you observe, think, and feel?

The Father honored the promise of the Son to send the Spirit to indwell these new Christians both individually and corporately. In other words, when I became a Christian, the Holy Spirit came to live within me, and He united me with a group of other people who have the Holy Spirit living in them. Together we are the temple of the Holy Spirit.

A church, then, is a group of people committed to Jesus Christ who are bound together by the indwelling influence of the Holy Spirit.

3. What do these Bible verses tell you about the church and your
   role in the church?

   a. 1 Corinthians 12:12–13

       My role:

   b. 1 Corinthians 12:27

       My role:

c. 1 Corinthians 14:26

    My role:

d. Ephesians 4:25

    My role:

The church was born on the first day of the Pentecost celebration in Jerusalem. Acts 2 gives a detailed, vivid account of these phenomena. After Peter had preached his Holy Spirit-inspired sermon, the people asked, "What shall we do to be saved?" Peter's reply and the reaction of the people are recorded in Acts 2:38–47.

1. What do these verses teach you about the very beginnings of the church?

    a. Acts 2:40

b. Acts 2:42

c. Acts 2:43

d. Acts 2:44–45

e. Acts 2:46–47

Acts 2:46 tells of two spheres of the early church. The first part of the verse tells of the "Big Church"—"So continuing daily with one accord in the temple." This was a large group of believers gathered in the temple to worship. The temple was a large place where hundreds and thousands could meet and worship.

That same thing happens today when crowds of people meet in churches to worship. They sing praises, pray together, hear God's Word, and glorify Jesus Christ. On some worship days, there may be baptisms or the Lord's Supper is observed—more opportunities to rejoice.

2. How is your church like the "Big Church"?

3. What element of the worship service is most meaningful to you? Why?

The second sphere of church life in Acts 2:46 can be called the "Small Church"—"and breaking bread from house to house, they ate their food with gladness and simplicity of heart." The believers not only met in huge numbers in the temple, but they also broke into smaller groups and met in each other's homes. That's where friendships were formed, where they could share their burdens and find help and support from each other.

In today's church, that is often done in adult Sunday School and smaller Bible study groups. In these small groups, people can best experience the care and love of other believers. Small groups are where prayer and pastoral care become personal, and each other's needs are met through the grace of God.

A couple of years ago, my wife and I vacationed in California and visited the national parks that are filled with redwood trees. They are so old that some were standing during the days of Christ, and they're considered the largest things on earth, towering hundreds of feet above the forest floor. You might think that trees that large would have a root system reaching hundreds of feet into the earth, but the redwoods actually have very shallow systems of roots. How can such tall trees remain upright when their root systems are relatively shallow?

According to the park guide, they all intertwine. They are locked to each other. When the storms come or the winds blow, the redwoods stand. Their roots are interlocked, and they don't stand-alone; all the trees support and protect each other. That's a picture of the relationships in "Small Church."

4. If you are part of a small group in your church, how does your participation enrich your worship life?

5. How does being part of a small group affect your everyday life?

1. Make a list of the three most important things your church offers you, or the three most important things you *want* from a church.

Remember, if you are looking for the perfect church, you will never find it; no church is perfect. And yes, it should not surprise you that every church has its share of hypocrites.

Every church is made up of people from various backgrounds, with different levels of maturity and different life experiences.

2. But we all have one thing in common! Read Romans 3:23 to discover what that is.

We are all sinners before God. We are forgiven, but we are not perfect and never will be this side of heaven.

Don't expect the church to be perfect; just get involved and help to make it better. Replace complaints about what you don't like or what doesn't meet your expectations with constructive ideas on how to improve those areas. Then help make it happen! Concentrating on the positive aspects of a church will help you as you work to make it live up to its promise.

3. What positive things did Paul tell the churches in these verses?

   a. Romans 1:7

   b. 1 Corinthians 1:2–4

   c. Philippians 1:1–6

d. Colossians 1:1–4

4. How can you follow Paul's example in interacting with the people in your church?

1. Read Acts 2:42 and Hebrews 10:24–25. What do you learn about faithfulness in the church?

In all areas of your church life, both "Big Church" and "Small Church," it is most important to be faithful—faithful in church attendance, faithful in physical, financial, and spiritual support, and faithful in making your church a place of worship and praise of our Savior, Jesus.

The Lord Jesus Christ died and rose again to create a group of people, redeemed by His blood, who love God and who love each other—and then He sent them out to win the world and to build the church together. Let every one of us be a part of it!

2. Write a prayer focused on how you can be a vital part of your church.

3. Write out Hebrews 10:25 and make it your memory verse for this week. How can you live out this verse?

As Week 4 ends, take time to write a prayer for your church or the church you desire to become part of soon.

Dear God,

In Jesus' name, Amen

week 5

Devotions: How Can I Stay Close to God?

Nothing is more important to the Christian than the practice of having a daily appointment with the Lord, a regular period of daily Bible study and prayer. Some people call this daily devotions. Others, the morning watch. Still others refer to their quiet time. It's the missing ingredient in many Christian's lives.

I'm grateful to the Lord for bringing several influences into my life that helped me establish this practice when I was younger. The first influence, though I wasn't fully conscious of it at the time, was my father. As I grew up, I'd often see him reading his Bible at night; and when I was barely old enough to read, he bought me a little Bible, which I kept beside my bed, and in this way I learned as a child to read the Scriptures daily.

That didn't mean, however, that I was actively having a meaningful quiet time, and as I grew older I got away from close daily fellowship with the Lord and grew confused in life, as young people often do. In 1971, I enrolled at Columbia Bible College in South Carolina, transferring there as a sophomore. On my second night in the dorms, I surrendered my life to the Lord, and during the following weeks, I began to learn the importance of quiet time.

In fact, at that time in the early 1970s, student life was regimented, and the daily quiet time was a required part of our schedule. A bell loud enough to call the fire department awakened us every morning at 6:15. We had a half-hour to shower, shave (or put on make-up, depending on which side of campus you lived), and dress; then another bell would ring, signaling our quiet time. We had half an hour every morning, from 6:45 to 7:15, then a third bell would clang, sending us to breakfast.

At first I wasn't too excited about the schedule. I liked to stay up late, and sometimes I'd slump over my desk during my quiet time in a dead sleep. Then one day a man came to preach in our chapel services, and I'd never heard anyone like him. He stood in the pulpit like a machine gun, his rapid fire, crystal-clear British accent delivering brilliant expositions of interesting passages of Scripture. One day after chapel I approached him—his name was Stephen Olford—and I asked him if he had any advice for a young man contemplating going into the ministry.

"Yes," said Dr. Olford, with the same dramatic delivery I'd heard in the pulpit. "Yes," he said, "I do. Never, never, never miss your quiet time."

That's all he said. But that was enough. I began to realize that there must be something pretty important about this half-hour between the bells.

1. Read Mark 1:35 and Matthew 6:6. What do you learn about the importance of devotions?

These verses are two examples of what the Bible says about daily devotions. Even though Jesus is God, He found a quiet, removed place to pray and talk to His Father each day. In the Matthew verse, Jesus was teaching us about praying and spending time with God. Both Bible verses speak of quiet and privacy. When we have our daily time with God, or devotions, it is important to minimize the outside distractions as much as possible so we can concentrate on our Bible reading, meditation, and prayer, and so we can listen to God speaking to us.

An Old Testament example of daily devotion over a long lifetime is found in Daniel 6:1–10. Daniel's enemies knew of his lifelong habit of daily prayer, and used that knowledge to try to trap him. Read the passage in Daniel and then answer the following.

2. Briefly describe the plan of Daniel's enemies (verse 1–9).

3. How did Daniel react to the law (verse 10)?

Another influence that impacted my commitment to daily quiet time greatly was my interest in Christian biography. Over and over as I read about the lives and ministries of great Christian men and women, I discovered they had one thing in common. They maintained a quiet time habit.

The great Puritan, **Thomas Watson**, wrote: "The best time to converse with God is before worldly occasions stand knocking at the door to be let in: The morning is, as it were, the cream of the day, let the cream be taken off, and let God have it. Wind up thy heart towards heaven at the beginning of the day, and it will go the better all the day after."[1]

Well-known British statesman, the late **Earl Cairns**, Lord Chancellor of England, was an extremely busy man, but no matter what time he reached home in the evening, he always arose at the same hour to have his quiet time the next morning. His wife said, "We would sometimes get home from Parliament at two o'clock in the morning, but Lord Cairns would always arise at the same hour to pray and study the Bible."[2] He later attributed his success in life to this practice.

A missionary to China, **Bertha Smith**, wrote an absolutely fascinating story of her life. It was bitterly cold in her part of China. During the day, she wore 30 pounds of clothing, and at night, she slept under heavy bedding and with a hot water bottle. But her challenge came in the early morning hour when she wanted to rise before others so she could have her quiet time before the scores of interruptions that each day brought. She would struggle in the darkness to put on her layers of clothing, and then break the ice to wash her face in the cold water. Slipping out to a particular haystack, she would rake aside the frosted part of the hay, kneel down, and spend time with the Lord before the sun came up.[3]

Of **Dr. Campbell Morgan**, I read: "Here was a man who coveted for himself a constant withdrawal from the pressing demands of his busy life, and kept inviolate the sanctity of the early morning vigil of prayer and meditation. Here he breathed the atmosphere of heaven, and daily recharged his spirit with the power that in turn poured out in extravagant measure in the preaching and proclamation of the Word."[4]

1. What did you find most intriguing or surprising about these Christians?

2. Which one most influenced your thinking about daily devotions? Why?

3. How can you implement their examples into your own devotional life?

notes

[1]Thomas Watson, *Gleanings from Thomas Watson*, (Morgan, PA: Soli Deo Gloria Publications [Ligonier Ministries], 1995, first published in London in 1915), p. 107.

[2]R. A. Torrey, *How to Succeed in the Christian Life* (Chicago: Moody Press, u.d.), p. 50.

[3]Bertha Smith, *Go Home and Tell* (Nashville: Broadman & Holman Publishers, 1995), p. 76.

[4]Jill Morgan, *A Man of the World: Life of G. Campbell Morgan* (Grand Rapids: Baker Book House, 1972), p. 342.

1. What do these Bible verses teach you about daily devotions?

    a. Psalm 119:15–16

b. Psalm 119:147–148

c. Matthew 14:23

d. 1 Thessalonians 5:16–18

It's important to realize that a daily quiet time does not represent the totality of our fellowship with God. It doesn't mean that we can meet God in the morning and then leave Him there in the closet while we go into the day. The Bible tells us to pray without ceasing. In other words, communion and fellowship with God is the constant privilege of the Christian.

It's also important to realize that a daily quiet time is not simply a routine or a ritual. It's a relationship. We meet Christ at the *cross,* and we call that *conversion.* We meet with Him in the *closet,* and we call that *conversation.* At the cross is where we come to *know Christ,* and in the closet is where we come to *know Him better.*

2. Read Exodus 33:11. How did Moses meet with the Lord?

The quiet time is essentially a conversation, a time of fellowship, a daily meeting or appointment with the Lord. It isn't a complicated thing, and the simpler we can keep it the better. It isn't even always necessary to have a Bible. Sometimes it's nice just to go for a walk and spend some time meditating on some verse of memorized Scripture, and then talking to the Lord about it and praying over the things that concern you.

Usually, however, it's very helpful to have a Bible. And remember that you aren't reading your Bible to get through a certain amount of Scripture or to prepare a sermon or to develop a Sunday School or Bible study lesson. You're going to the Bible in order to find nourishment for your soul.

3. Write out Psalm 37:3–4 and memorize it!

follow a two-step plan—Scripture and prayer. It's my **procedure** for my devotions. I take whatever verses I'm reading that day and meditate on it (really think about it). And then I use those verses in my prayer. That's the essence of it—a time of Bible reading and meditation followed by a time of prayer. It's conversation. The Lord speaks to me through His Word, then I speak to Him through prayer. And it's through this sort of daily conversation that we get to know Him better.

1. What benefits are there to having "conversation" with God through Bible reading and prayer? Where will you start reading?

Another influence came into my life, an older woman who was well-known for her wit and wisdom, Mrs. Ruth Bell Graham. One day she said, "Robert, do you have the notebook habit?" I didn't know what the notebook habit was, so I said no, I didn't think I did. She told me about her little loose-leaf notebook made of leather. She said she kept wearing it out, but she had a leather crafter who kept repairing it for her.

In her little notebook, she would record the insights God gave her each day as she studied her Bible. That very day I drove into town, found a stationary shop, and bought a notebook, and began using it as a sort of journal for my quiet time, a practice that I've followed ever since.

This notebook can be a personal summary of what is happening in your life and how you are communicating with God. The notebook can be divided into two sections—the first part can be a journal where you record something about your day, how you are feeling, the Scripture reference you're reading, and some new understandings you may have gained. The second half of the notebook can be used for prayer lists.

Find a regular place and time. Jesus used different places for His quiet time. Mark 1:35 tells us Jesus went "to a solitary place." Matthew 14:23 tells us Jesus went "up on the mountain by Himself to pray." After the Last Supper, Jesus went to the Garden of Gethsemane to pray. For you the place may be your bedside, a quiet corner of your garden, or the front seat of your car.

2. Where will your regular place be?

3. What time of day will you have your devotions?

Persevere. Hang in there. At first, it may seem stiff and awkward; you might even wonder if you're getting much out of it. Don't give up. On some days my quiet time is more meaningful than others, but it's worthwhile every day, and if I miss a day of meeting with the Lord in prayer and Bible reading, it seems as if my entire day is off-kilter.

I read about an exploring party in Africa that was pushing with great intensity through the jungle and the bush. After making remarkable progress, the explorer grew frustrated when his national guides just sat down and refused to go further. He asked, "Are you tired?" Not particularly.

"Are you sick?" No.

"Well, why have you stopped?"

Their answer was, "We must pause now to let our souls catch up with our bodies."

Why not begin the practice of daily devotions tomorrow? Better yet, why not start today!

1. Using the suggestions offered in this week's study, make your own personal commitment to daily devotions below. Be specific!

2. For your Simple memory, write out and memorize Psalm 119:147–148.

As we finish Week 5, write out a prayer asking for guidance as you strive to grow in faith and understanding through your devotions.

Dear God,

In Jesus' name, Amen

week 6

Evangelism: How Can I Share My Faith with Others?

While visiting a particular city, Katrina and I took a taxi, and we soon learned our driver was a Muslim gentleman from Africa. As we chatted with him, I sought to bring up the subject of Christianity and he commented there was little difference between Christianity and Islam. "Really there are only two differences," he said. "Muslims don't believe that God had a son, and Muslims don't eat pork."

Being a little surprised at his naiveté, I suggested there might be some other differences. "Like what?" he asked.

"Well, for one thing," I said, pausing to choose my words, "Mohammad is dead, and Jesus Christ is alive. He rose from the grave on the third day."

My taxi driver nodded thoughtfully and admitted that was a significant difference. And I felt the Lord had given me an opportunity to gently plant a seed of truth in the man's mind.

Christians are like Johnny Appleseed. We go through each day looking for quiet ways to sow the seed of the gospel; and that is the meaning of evangelism. The very word *evangelism* is wonderful. The prefix, *ev*, means *good*. And the stem word is *angel*. We think of an angel as a supernatural being, but the original meaning was simply "messenger."

So the word *ev-angel-ism* is literally *good-message-ism*, and the word *evangelist* refers to anyone who shares the Good News with another.

1. Read Mark 1:16–18 and John 1:43–45. What are your observations about evangelism from these passages?

In the passage above from Mark, we see one command—not two. Jesus didn't say, "Follow Me and fish for men." He said, "Follow Me, and *I will make you* become fishers of men." Jesus is telling His disciples—and that means us as well—that we are to follow Him and *He* will make us fishers of men. We don't need to do this on our own, for that could be very intimidating. And we could never by our own personality or persuasiveness change another person's heart—only Jesus can do that.

When Jesus met the men mentioned in the above Bible verses, they were fishermen—not evangelists. They believed in Jesus as their Savior and followed Him, but they made many mistakes and missteps. They often lacked faith and were plagued by doubts. They didn't understand everything Jesus had taught them. (You can read about these incidents throughout the gospel accounts.) Yet in Acts 4, we discover that these same men became evangelists and preached the gospel before a hostile Jewish ruling council with strength, with compassion, and with authority.

2. How did Peter act as an evangelist in Acts 4:12?

3. How did the listeners react in Acts 4:13?

Christians experience the same pattern. First, we become followers. Then Jesus makes us fishers of men and women—evangelists. As we grow in our own faith we can, with the Holy Spirit's help, become more influential in leading others to Christ.

4. What do these verses say about "fishing for men"?

    a. Luke 5:10

    b. 2 Timothy 2:24–26

We must be aware that we're not the only ones interested in catching fish. The New Testament was originally written in the Greek language. There is a word that only occurs twice in the Greek New Testament, the word *zogreo* (zo-gre'-o). It means "to catch, like in a net."

We first encounter the word *zogreo* in Luke 5. Here Jesus had been teaching the multitudes. The crowds were so great that Jesus got into a boat, pushed out from the shore, and taught the multitudes from the water. Then, His teaching finished for the moment, Jesus told Peter to launch further into the lake and to let down his nets. Suddenly so many fish swam into the nets that the boats were in danger of sinking.

Take a moment to read Luke 5:1–11 and then answer the following questions:

1. What was Simon Peter's reaction (Luke 5:8–10)?

2. What was Jesus' instruction?

This was a rephrasing of our Lord's promise to make Peter and the other disciples into fishers of men. You will catch (*zogreo*) men in the nets of the gospel.

3. This unusual word occurs one other time in the Bible, in 2 Timothy 2:24–26. What are the details of the apostle's instruction to Timothy about his ministry?

This word, which means to catch in a trap or in a net, occurs only twice in the New Testament. The Holy Spirit put it there to show us we're to be diligently fishing for men, for another fisherman—a diabolical personage of evil—is also trolling for men, women, boys, and girls, and he wants to catch them in his snares.

4. Who do you know that needs to know about salvation in Jesus?

5. How do you feel about telling that person about Christ?

6. What are some of your concerns and fears?

7. What is your reaction to Jesus' promises concerning evangelism?

How do we become fishers of men doing the work of evangelism? How can we influence others to come to Christ?

1. Write out 1 Peter 3:15.

There should be such joy and hope in our **attitude** because of Christ that it is evident to those around us. When others ask why we have such an upbeat attitude or why we are hopeful in difficult situations, it gives us an opportunity to share the gospel. Our attitude often precedes our words about Jesus.

2. How would you describe your attitude right now?

3. How do you show that attitude at home, with friends, or in the workplace? Think of someone who may be influenced by your attitude?

4. What do these verses teach about being an effective witness for Christ?

    a. Matthew 5:16

b. John 13:35

The most powerful kind of witness are those good deeds and acts of kindness that communicate the love of Jesus Christ to another person.

We witness by our assertiveness. While it's essential to witness by our attitudes and by our actions, sooner or later it's necessary for us to actually say a word for the Lord. We have to communicate the message of Christ by lip. It might be in the form of a simple sentence about Christ. It might be in a note or in a letter. It might be simply inviting someone to church or to an evangelistic event; but sooner or later we have to be assertive about our faith.

Admittedly, this isn't very popular in our culture today because it isn't considered "politically correct" to share our faith with unbelievers. But then, it's never been popular with the world when Christians share their faith. In the book of Acts, the Jewish Sanhedrin commanded those first apostles to shut up, to no longer preach in the name of Christ. "Don't evangelize," they said. "Don't tell others about your faith. Don't try to persuade someone else."

5. How did Peter answer this?

   a. Acts 5:29

   b. Acts 4:19–20

6. What is holding you back from telling others about Jesus?

When you invite someone to church, take them to a gospel service, or say a word for the Lord, you never know how God may use that in another person's life. Only in heaven will we see the full measure of our work for the Lord. But there comes a time when we have to be assertive in sharing our faith, for the love of Christ compels us to do so.

And sometimes we have to keep telling them again and again. That doesn't mean we have to be great preachers or world famous evangelists. An evangelist is one who shares the Good News of Christ whether the audience is a great multitude in a stadium or one child sitting on our patio.

1. What is the key element, basic foundation for sharing your faith with others? Read Matthew 28:19–20; Luke 19:10; and Acts 1:8 for the answer.

The Holy Spirit will guide you as you evangelize. We have the promise of God's ever-helpful presence. And because of that, we also follow God's command to pursue Him, to know more about Him, and thus be prepared when opportunities arise—or when we create opportunities—to share God's goodness with others. We can obey God's command to share *because* God enables us to do it.

2. Who will you tell about Christ's work in your life?

3. What will you say?

An old mission hymn, "Hark the Voice of Jesus Calling," written by Daniel March (1868), gives a clear picture of what you can do to share your faith. A verse of the hymn says:

If you cannot speak like angels,
If you cannot preach like Paul,
You can tell the love of Jesus,
You can say he died for all.
If you cannot rouse the wicked
With the judgment's dread alarms,
You can lead the little children
To the Savior's waiting arms.

People everywhere need to have Christ in their lives. You may be the one to plant a seed with your co-worker, your child's teacher, or someone in your family. Look for opportunities each day.

1. What Bible verses are significant to you? How can you share those with others as an encouragement?

2. How has God's redemption changed your life? How can you share that story with others?

3. Write out a verse you have read in Week 6 and make it your new memory verse, asking God to continue to equip you to share His love with others.

As Week 6 comes to a close, I suggest you first make a list of others you desire to share your faith with in the coming days. Then write a prayer asking for opportunity and boldness to share the wonderful news so many need to hear of the simple faith offered by Jesus Christ.

I want to share my faith with:

Dear God,

In Jesus' name, Amen

note to
LEADERS

Visit **www.randallhouse.com** and receive a free *Leader's Guide for Simple Small Group Study.* Discover tools to aid you in leading your church or small study group through a six-week journey that explains the ABC's of the Christian faith.

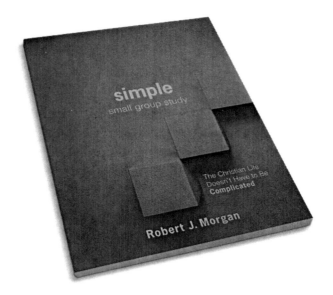

To order additional copies of *Simple Small Group Study* call 1-800-877-7030 or log onto **www.randallhouse.com**.

Quantity discount for 24 or more copies at $8.99 each.

D6 Devotional Magazines

for the entire family!

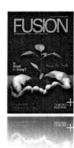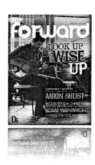

D6 Devotional Magazines are unique because they are the only brand of devotional magazines where the entire family studies the same Bible theme at the same time.

Think about how long it would take you to track down all of the resources for each member of your family to connect with God on the same topic. Who has that kind of time? We do! It's not that we have nothing else to do, we are just passionate about D6. So look no further, we have created the resource for which you are looking, and it works!

D6 Devotional Magazines are full-color, interactive, fun, and exciting tools to connect with God and with each other.

Subscribe now!

800.877.7030

D6family.com

D6 | Conference

a conversation. a platform. a gathering.

Bridging churches and homes
to the **heart of Deuteronomy 6.**

Volunteers
Deuteronomy 6 Young Adult Ministry Dad **Student Ministry**
@theD6conference Family-Based Youth Ministry @theD6confere
Generational Discipleship Family Worship at Home
#FamMin Faith@Home Parenting Mom Research **Worship**
Pastors Lead Pastor **Spiritual Formation** #KidMin @D6family
Mothers #KidMin @theD6conference
The Gospel **Family Ministry** #FamMin **Dads, Fathers, Husbands** Biblical Discipleship
Research Discipleship @theD6conference **Strategy**
onference **Church Fathers MOM Deut. 6** Blended Family **Church + Home**
family Creative **Dad** #StuMin Influence @theD6conference
Biblical Discipleship Volunteers **Children's Minstry** **Lead Pastor**
Parents @theD6conference Women's Ministry

Connect with us online
D6conference.com

DON'T LET FEAR HOLD YOU BACK.

MOVE BEYOND THE PAIN AND STEP OUT INTO FREEDOM.

The author shares details concerning the **emotional and physical symptoms** related to the subject as well as ways to overcome these difficulties.

Readers will find **words of comfort and hope** through Scripture, examples from the Bible of those dealing with difficulties, and practical advice on surviving the difficult situation they are facing.

A **list of resources** is given to encourage further help where needed.

CPSIA information can be obtained at www.ICGtesting.com
Printed in the USA
LVOW11s1011200913

352837LV00004B/4/P